The

HIDDEN MICKEYS

of DISNEYLAND

Written by BILL SCOLLON

EDITIONS

LOS ANGELES ❤ NEW YORK

CONTENTS

DISNEY CALIFORNIA ADVENTURE PARK

INTRODUCTION

"The thing that's going to make Disneyland unique and different is the detail. If we lose the detail, we lose it all."

— **WALT DISNEY**

During the construction of Disneyland, Walt Disney and his team of artists and designers understood that details and flourishes would heighten the Guest experience. Among those touches was the addition of names painted on the windows of Main Street, U.S.A. honoring people who helped bring Disneyland to life. The names go unnoticed by thousands of Guests everyday, but for those who know a bit about the park's history, the hidden names are a special touch.

Hidden Mickeys are like that, too. They're details that bring another layer of entertainment to the park. Hidden Mickeys began to appear in the 1980s, and there are plenty of opinions about what makes a true Hidden Mickey. For our purposes, a Hidden Mickey is:

 A three-circle silhouette or outline of Mickey Mouse's head composed of a larger, central circle and smaller circles for ears, attached in the right spots. The ears can also be detached, as long as they're not too far away from the head. However, Mickey's head does not have to be right-side-up; it can be upside down or sideways.

- 🐭 A profile of Mickey Mouse's head
- 🐭 A full-body outline or silhouette of Mickey Mouse
- 🐭 A full-color drawing of Mickey Mouse

True Hidden Mickeys are those that have been intentionally placed and are somewhat hard to find. There are hundreds of obvious Mickeys but you have to work to discover a Hidden Mickey. That said, throughout this book, you will find exceptions— Hidden Mickeys that don't quite fit the criteria but are too good to pass up. One other note: this book does not include Mickey Mouse seen in shows, parades, and other amusements that can be expected to change regularly. Hidden Mickeys should be somewhat permanent.

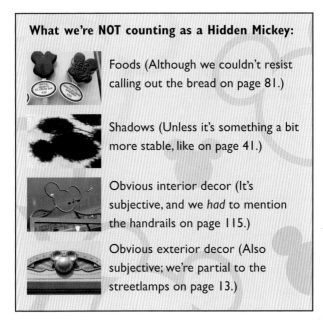

What we're NOT counting as a Hidden Mickey:

Foods (Although we couldn't resist calling out the bread on page 81.)

Shadows (Unless it's something a bit more stable, like on page 41.)

Obvious interior decor (It's subjective, and we *had* to mention the handrails on page 115.)

Obvious exterior decor (Also subjective; we're partial to the streetlamps on page 13.)

WHO'S THE LEADER OF THE BAND?

The largest Hidden Mickey is one you won't be able to see for yourself . . . unless you're in an airplane! If you're strolling along the sidewalks of South Disneyland Drive (away from Disney's Paradise Pier Hotel and toward West Katella Avenue), you might notice that the pavement rounds some gardens. When viewed from above, the sidewalks form a classic Hidden Mickey. Take a look at certain maps throughout the resort, and you might catch artistic renderings too.

Of course, any Hidden Mickey can disappear when attractions are refurbished. So, if you can't find a particular one, it may be because it's gone. The good news is that new Hidden Mickeys are added from time to time, so keep your eyes open!

This book is organized by area. The names of attractions, shops, and restaurants are listed alphabetically. The first part of each entry gives general information about the location of a Hidden Mickey, while the last lines—in italics—are more specific. So, if you only want a hint, don't read the italicized lines!

To put this guide together, I consulted other publications and websites, did research at the Walt Disney Archives, interviewed Cast Members, and searched the resort. A special thanks goes to my wife, Barbara, for helping me scour the parks, stores, and hotels for days.

Have fun!

— *Bill Scollon*

 P. S. Keep a sharp eye out for this icon on certain entries, earmarking the hardest-to-spot Hidden Mickeys.

DISNEYLAND PARK

MAIN STREET, U.S.A.

Main Street, U.S.A. evokes the spirit of small-town America—like Walt Disney's childhood home of Marceline, Missouri—at the beginning of the twentieth century. Be sure to take note of the names painted on windows. They pay tribute to those who helped make Disneyland a reality.

YOUR FIRST STOP

👍 Your day at one (or both!) of the parks begins with a quick bag check at security. While there, take a look at the pictures hanging overhead. They hold safety messages from Pumbaa and Timon. At least two of them have Hidden Mickeys and a few others have obvious Mickeys. (Note: You can't see all the signs from one security line.)

Find the sign that reads, HOLD ON TO YOUR GEAR! There's a Hidden Mickey key ring among the items that are blowing out of the roller coaster.

Another sign reads, LET THE CUBS DECIDE IF THEY WANT TO RIDE. A Hidden Mickey appears as a reflection on the hood of the ride vehicle.

PLAZA

👆 **Benches:** Somewhere in the plaza, Mickey is just sitting around.

Near the right side of Disneyland Park's main entrance, look for benches with concrete Mickey shapes holding up each end.

Bricks: As you walk across the plaza, notice the personalized paving bricks under your feet. Can you find four different types of Hidden Mickeys on the bricks?

A classic Hidden Mickey within a bell

An outline of Mickey with his arms out

A hint of mouse ears above a circle

An outline of Mickey's head

Mosaic: Right in the middle of the plaza is a large compass mosaic. These Hidden Mickeys here are pretty obvious, as long as you look down!

Four Hidden Mickeys are grouped in the center.

Signposts: There are several directional signposts here and at other parts of the resort area. Look for Hidden Mickeys, high and low.

On top is a classic Hidden Mickey. It's fairly obvious, but only if you're looking up!

Look at the base. Classic Hidden Mickeys are part of the embossed design.

Streetlamps: If you arrive on the tram from the parking garage, take a look at the streetlamps. They appear in other parts of the resort, too.

There is a classic Hidden Mickey finial on top.

Ticket booths: Examine the ticket booths outside the main gate. Mickey is being very supportive.

Beneath the counters are brackets with classic Hidden Mickey cutouts.

A REAL TUFFY **Tree enclosures:** As you walk into the plaza, note the green metal tree enclosures. There is something very Mickey Mouse about the way they're held together.

The rivets are in the shape of a classic Hidden Mickey.

ENTRY GATE

Costumes: Check out the costumes worn by the Cast Members at the main gate. Small, round Hidden Mickeys are part of their ensemble.

Profile Hidden Mickeys are embossed on the brass buttons. Keep an eye out for Hidden Mickeys on other Cast Member costumes throughout the park.

Turnstile: As soon as you enter the park, turn around and look at where the Cast Members are working. See anything?

Classic Hidden Mickeys are on the backs of the turnstiles.

MAIN STREET, U.S.A.

👍 **The Book Rest:** At least one Hidden Mickey rests in each window scene.

> *Look for a red-and-gold book spine, and find Mickey in the upper center.*

👉 **City Hall:** As you stand in the Town Square facing the castle, City Hall is to your left. Two Hidden Mickeys may be waving to you!

> *Mickey is on flags that sit above both wings of the City Hall building. If there's a breeze, he's waving!*

👍 **Disneyland Casting Agency door:** This decorative door boasts two Hidden Mickeys.

> *They are both part of the border design, top and bottom.*

👍 **Disneyland Railroad station:** Walt Disney loved trains, and the railway has been part of the park since opening day. Face the station and see if you can spot the Hidden Mickey.

> *He's on flags above the station.*

👉 **Emporium:** From the street, see if you can spot a Hidden Mickey in the display windows.

The outline of a classic Hidden Mickey forms the top of wire-frame book stands.

 Emporium: Inside, behind a cash register, is a painted mural featuring flowers in vases and a fantastic hard-to-find Mickey.

A blue glass ball sits on the small table. In it is a silhouette of Mickey in his "Sorcerer's Apprentice" outfit from Fantasia, *and he's holding a wand. If you spotted it, you're good!*

Fruit cart: Find the fresh-fruit cart about halfway down Main Street, U.S.A. The fruit on top looks delicious, but what's down below?

There's a classic Hidden Mickey incorporated into the metal framework underneath.

Main Street Cinema: This is a cool place to visit when it's hot outside! Mickey lights the way.

Small Mickey-shaped lights illuminate the stairs.

Main Street Magic Shop: From the street, check the display window. See if you can spot a first-rate Hidden Mickey in a rectangle.

*Look for a playing card—
the Ace of Mickeys!*

👆 **Main Street Magic Shop:**
Walk into the shop and look up.

*Another Ace of Mickeys
is on the ceiling.*

👍 **Main Street Magic Shop:** A Hidden Mickey lies inside a velvety display case.

A magic rope is coiled into a classic Hidden Mickey.

👉 **Penny Arcade:** Look for the old-fashioned Pinocchio game machine. Want to play? Mickey does!

A classic Hidden Mickey is situated between the orange buttons on the machine.

👆 **Main Street Photo Supply:** Focus on the old cameras on display for a picture-perfect Mickey.

Two small dials and the camera's lens form a classic Hidden Mickey, turned sideways.

👍 **Plaza Inn restaurant:** A rosy Mickey, rotated to one side, can be found in a still life, to the right of the right-hand cashiers.

A painting of roses has a pretty good Mickey, turned clockwise about ninety degrees, all done in flowers.

FANTASYLAND

Step through Sleeping Beauty

Castle into the heart of

Disneyland. In front of you is the

King Arthur Carrousel. Built in

1922, it was purchased from an

amusement park in Canada. Each

horse is a hand-carved antique!

👍 **Alice in Wonderland:** In the room where cards paint the roses red, look for a Hidden Mickey in the hedge.

A red paint splotch near a heart-shaped topiary is most certainly Mickey's head.

👉 **Casey Jr. Circus Train:** The engineer drives the train from inside the locomotive. Is there a helpful Hidden Mickey aboard?

Three dials on the engineer's control panel form a Hidden Mickey. You can see it from behind the railing or from various points in the queue.

🖐 **Castle Heraldry Shoppe:** Find the mailbox outside this shop near the castle.

Several Hidden Mickeys wearing sorcerer hats branch off from the trellis pattern along the top and bottom, and a classic Hidden Mickey adorns the middle of the bottom trellis.

👍 **Castle Heraldry Shoppe:** Browse the shop until you gaze upon a vase with three grapes forming a familiar shape.

A vase, up on a shelf near the back of the store, has a Hidden Mickey at the bottom of a bunch of grapes.

A REAL TUFFY **"it's a small world":** Outside the attraction, Cast Members keep things under control from three raised platforms.

The three round elevated platforms make a classic Hidden Mickey. If you were hovering above the ground, it would be easier to see! (You can also check out the satellite view from your home computer.)

👉 **King Arthur Carrousel:** Jingles, the carousel's lead horse, is easy to spot by the rows of bells hanging on him. Is Mickey riding along?

Three jewels suggest a three-circle Mickey, but the ears are set pretty far above the head. Is this a true Hidden Mickey or an accidental Mickey? You decide!

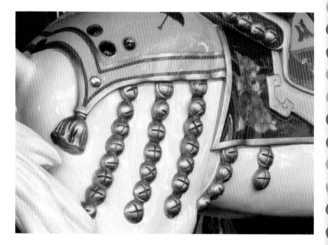

🖐 **Mad Hatter Shop:** Any sign of a Hidden Mickey here?

Look up at the sign above the door. Mickey ears are on the right.

Matterhorn Bobsleds: In the covered area of the queue, look to your right and search the coats of arms that hang near the ceiling.

Find the red-and-white coat of arms that has a design that resembles a key. A small Mickey is just below the midline, in the center. If you found this on your own, congratulations!

 Mr. Toad's Wild Ride: On the ride, as you pass through Winky's Pub, take a look at the foam on the spinning mug on the left.

Did you see a Hidden Mickey in the bubbles of foam? It's a tough one, and it goes by really fast.

☞ **Peter Pan's Flight:** From outside the ride, look up at the windows on the second floor. Is Mickey hidden there?

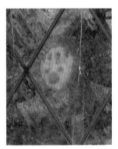

A teddy bear sits in the window on the right. Hidden Mickeys are on the bottom of his feet.

 Peter Pan's Flight: On the ride, as you fly over London, pay attention to Big Ben. Someone is peering out of a window.

This is a great one. A profile of Mickey is in one of the windows as you move around the back of Big Ben. A really super Hidden Mickey!

👆 **Pinocchio's Daring Journey:** As you get close to the loading zone, check out the painting on the wall for a series of Hidden Mickeys.

The circles on window shutters above the loading zone have a fairly good head-to-ears ratio.

A REAL TUFFY **Pinocchio's Daring Journey:** As you pass through the Pleasure Island part of the ride, you'll see a popcorn machine and popcorn spilled on the ground. Can you pick out Mickey?

Another tough one. There are many circular shapes, and you pass by it really fast. Good luck!

Pinocchio's Daring Journey: As you pass through Geppetto's house, watch for a bookcase with a ship model displayed on top of it.

The wooden frame surrounding the case holding the ship features a classic Hidden Mickey.

Pinocchio's Daring Journey: Watch for a juggling clown and look at the balls painted on the wall on the right.

Three balls form a not-quite-perfect Mickey.

Pixie Hollow: A wooden sign declares FAIRIES WELCOME. Mickey is welcome, too!

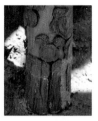

> *At the bottom of the wooden post is a perfect classic Hidden Mickey made out of tree bark.*

Snow White's Scary Adventures: As the ride vehicles leave the loading area, they turn right past a large mural. Keep an eye on the foliage.

> *Three trees form a pretty clear Mickey. You can see it just before you go through the first set of doors.*

 Snow White's Scary Adventures: On the left, after the mine, you'll see barrels full of gems. Any Mickeys hidden there?

> *This one is iffy. Some feel the three red gems form a Hidden Mickey. You decide— true Mickey or wannabe Mickey?*

A REAL TUFFY **Storybook Land Canal Boats:** You can watch from the railing as the beautiful boats head off on their tour. There are Hidden Mickeys on at least two of them.

Look for the boat named Wendy. *A classic Hidden Mickey is on the back, above the rudder.*

The lavender Mickey is to the right of the name Flora, *in the center of painted vines and flowers.*

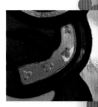

Village Haus Restaurant: The restaurant has beautiful stained glass windows. One, to the left of the main entrance, features a certain famous puppet and a number of Hidden Mickeys.

Look for Pinocchio. The stripe on his shorts is decorated with classic Hidden Mickeys. Very fashionable!

Village Haus Restaurant: Inside, to the right of the ordering counters, is a large mural of delicious

vegetables and fruit. With all those grapes and cherries, you're bound to harvest at least one Mickey.

A three-grape Mickey sits on the tip of the banana farthest to the right. Looks good enough to eat!

A REAL TUFFY **Village Haus Restaurant:** Ahoy! A model sailing ship sits on a shelf in the dining area. It tends to get moved from shelf to shelf. If you can find it, a classic Hidden Mickey awaits.

The Hidden Mickey is painted on the back, or stern, of the ship. If the back of the ship is to the wall, you may not be able to see it.

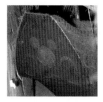

MICKEY'S TOONTOWN

According to Disney lore, Mickey's Toontown existed long before it opened in 1993. But Mickey and the other toon-folk asked Walt to keep it secret. At long last, the residents decided to open their community to the park's Guests. It is home to Mickey, Minnie, Donald, Chip and Dale, Goofy, and lots of Hidden Mickeys.

👍 **Clarabelle's Frozen Yogurt:** Clarabelle's icy treats are *moo*-velous. But when her stand is closed, a Hidden Mickey is revealed.

> *The pull-down metal shade is decorated with a cow-spot Mickey.*

👆 **Entrance Gate:** The B.P.O.M. welcomes you to Mickey's Toontown. Find out what that means and you'll find something else, too!

> *A sign for the Benevolent & Protective Order of Mouse proudly sits above the gated entrance to Mickey's Toontown. A classic Hidden Mickey is in the center.*

Fire Department: When you ring the bell, a Dalmatian looks out of the second-floor window to see who it is. Dalmatians have spots. Get the hint?

> *A three-circle Mickey, with the ears a bit too small and set apart, is turned sideways, at the top of the pup's forehead.*

Gadget's Go Coaster: You won't have to walk far down the queue to spot this rocky Hidden Mickey.

In the rock wall along the walkway, at the first turn, is a Hidden Mickey made of stones. It's not perfect, but it is clearly intentional.

Mickey's House: As you would expect, this house is packed with Hidden Mickeys. Many are pretty obvious, such as the front door and WELCOME mat, but some are harder to spot. To get started, check out the books in the first room.

There is a profile silhouette of Mickey on the spine of a blue book.

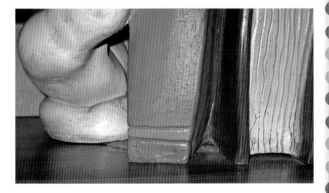

Mickey's House: Bookshelves in the second room are a good place to look, too.

A large book inside the bookcase on the right with the title My Life with Walt has a classic Hidden Mickey on its spine, too.

MOUSEWAY

Mickey's House: Mickey's player piano is a toon-ful spot to look for a hidden you-know-what.

Classic Mickey-shaped holes are punched into the player piano's scroll.

Mickey's House: A classic Hidden Mickey helps piano players keep the beat.

A Hidden Mickey is on the metronome sitting atop the piano.

Mickey's House: A fireplace keeps the next room warm and cozy. Perfect for curling up with a good book or two.

Across from the easy chair (featuring some obvious Mickeys), the bookshelf contains two more books with Mickey on their spine.

👆 **Mickey's House:** Look for the drums inside Mickey's Movie Barn. How does Mickey tighten the drumhead?

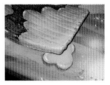

The adjustment knobs sport a set of Mickey ears!

A REAL TUFFY **Mickey's House:** In the prop room, a large mirror with the zodiac on its frame leans against the wall. Take a look—and be patient!

Every so often, Mickey's face appears.

👍 **Mickey's House:** In Donald's painting area, paint splotches are everywhere. Two brushes have the splotches you're looking for.

On the front counter, a brush with green paint partially covers a green Mickey, peeking out from the corner of the brush.

Another brush is covered with red spots. Three of them make a nice upside-down Mickey.

👆 **Mickey's House:** Outside, get an angle on the lamps by the driveway.

A classic Hidden Mickey is revealed when you view the lamps on the diagonal.

 Mickey's House: Mickey's bright red car sits out front. It's adorned with five somewhat Hidden Mickeys.

Look on each hubcap. Don't forget the spare tire!

A REAL TUFFY **Minnie's House:** Mickey's neighbor has her own set of Hidden Mickeys. Check out the books in the first room.

A book spine features a Hidden Mickey attached to the international symbol for woman. Clever!

Minnie's House: There are a couple of pictures of Mickey. Can you find them both?

There's a picture of Mickey with a fishing pole—and fish!—sitting on the fireplace mantel.

A picture of Mickey and Minnie together is in the second room.

Minnie's House: While you're snooping around the kitchen, take a look inside the refrigerator.

Minnie has a jar of cheese relish in the door with a classic Hidden Mickey on the label. An obvious, but sweet, Mickey magnet rests on the outside door, too.

Post Office: Look carefully at the sign above the post office that looks like a stamped letter.

A full-color drawing of mail carrier Mickey is on the stamp. He's also on the flag above.

A REAL TUFFY **Roger Rabbit's Car Toon Spin:** Along the queue, look for a barrel covered in paint swirls. Next to it is a large paintbrush.

A not-so-perfect Hidden Mickey, in white, is on the bristles of the brush.

 **Signpost:** Look for the directional sign near the Jolly Trolley station. Who's that walking along the top?

A full-figured silhouette of Mickey is striding across the top of the sign.

Toonhole cover: Two of these are found in the streets of Mickey's Toontown. One is near Goofy's Playhouse and the other is across from the Fire Department.

Mickey is cast in the center of the cover.

TOMORROWLAND

This land has undergone more makeovers than any other. After all, tomorrow quickly becomes today! Look for the rocket that sits on a roof near Space Mountain. It's a replica of the original Moonliner that served as the centerpiece of Tomorrowland for Disneyland's first dozen years.

👍 **Autopia:** Tailgating is never a good idea, but if you get close enough to the car ahead, you might see this Hidden Mickey.

Also visible from the loading area, a small classic Hidden Mickey is depicted on the sticker on the upper right corner of each license plate.

👉 **Buzz Lightyear Astro Blasters:** Planets of the Galactic Alliance are featured on maps and posters in the queue area. Look for a Mickey-shaped continent and classic Hidden Mickeys in planet clusters.

A continent on planet Ska-densii resembles the shape of Mickey's profile.

You can also find classic Hidden Mickeys in two clusters: K'lifooel'ch and the K'tleendon Kan Cluster.

Buzz Lightyear Astro Blasters: Outside the attraction, take a look at the large mural that wraps around the building. Rockets streak over an orange moon. But there's something mousy about one of the moon bases. . . .

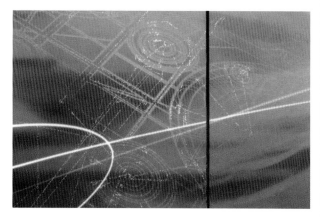

A schematic drawing of a base forms a partial classic Hidden Mickey.

A REAL TUFFY **Innoventions:** Check out the globe on the second floor. Keep your eyes on the lower third of the globe to see what bubbles up.

A classic Hidden Mickey composed of three bubbles moves past, going left to right. Watch for the scuba diver.

A REAL TUFFY **Innoventions:** Stand right in front of the globe, in the middle. Look down. Under the glass panels you're standing on are thousands of blue beads. Yep, you guessed it. Somewhere among them are two Hidden Mickeys!

Step back a bit. There are three red beads that make a super Hidden Mickey. Feel free to ask a Cast Member for help!

Another Hidden Mickey, made out of gray beads, is under a panel on the far left, two glass panels away from the wall. Good luck!

👍 **Innoventions:** Find the "outside" front door and see if you can find Mickey welcoming residents home.

Several classic Hidden Mickeys are hidden in the metal railings.

👉 **Innoventions:** Downstairs in the Innoventions Dream Home, there is a section of carpet you'll want to check out.

A pattern of gold interlocking circles creates a classic Hidden Mickey with one ear a bit above the head.

👍 **Innoventions:** The boy's bedroom has a Peter Pan storytelling attraction and two Hidden Mickeys.

Video projections appear on the screen and in windows around the room. In the presentation, watch the window closest to the stage for a Mickey-shaped cloud.

A bookshelf sports a Hidden Mickey bookend.

👍 **Innoventions:** As you exit Innoventions, on the outside first-floor walkway, look right to find a Hidden Mickey in the wall art around a set of double doors.

A large classic Hidden Mickey is above and to the left of the doors. Pretty obvious, right? But did you also see the partial Hidden Mickey painted on the doors?

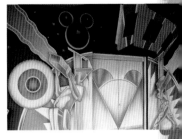

Platform tower: Face the TomorrowLanding shop, and look up at the satellite dishes. Position yourself just right to see an upside-down Hidden Mickey. To catch Mickey right side up, walk to the second level of the Innoventions entrance ramp.

Three satellite dishes are arranged to make a classic Hidden Mickey.

👍 **Space Mountain:** From the elevated section of the queue, see if you can spot Hidden Mickeys on the ride vehicle.

In every row, the center set of speakers is in the shape of Mickey's head.

👆 **Star Tours—The Adventures Continue:** In the first room of the queue, look for the computer panel behind C-3P0.

Two smaller circles and a bigger half circle at the center base of the panel look quite reminiscent.

✌ **Star Tours—The Adventures Continue:** Off to the right of the second room, look for the shadow of a droid wearing unusual headgear.

The droid has what appear to be Mickey ears above his head.

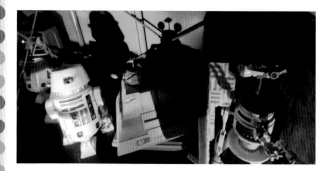

A REAL TUFFY **Star Tours—The Adventures Continue:** A large screen positioned above a tight turn in the queue shows the shadows of space travelers walking by. Keep your eyes peeled for R2-D2.

Catch R2-D2 in mouse ears. But he doesn't come by very often, so don't be disappointed if you don't see him.

👍 **Star Tours—The Adventures Continue:** On the left, find the droid who is scanning baggage and keep your eyes on the images in the scanner.

One of the x-ray images reveals a Mickey Mouse plush in a suitcase. But this is a fleeting image and easy to miss as you walk by.

👉 **The Star Trader store:** Find Hidden Mickeys in the room nearest to Space Mountain's exit.

Look for red atom-like spheres on the top of several displays.

ADVENTURELAND

The Jungle Cruise has been the centerpiece of Adventureland since Disneyland opened. The attraction is one of the best examples of the amazing landscaping skills of Disney Imagineers. As Guests wend their way through deep jungles, they have no idea that part of the ride is only about thirty-five feet from Main Street, U.S.A.!

👍 **Indiana Jones Adventure:** In the queue, in the room where the movie plays, there is a huge Hidden Mickey hiding in plain sight. Check between the lamps hanging on the left wall!

Between the last two lamps that are closest to the movie screen is a large, shadowy classic Hidden Mickey.

👉 **Indiana Jones Adventure:** As you pass by an office area, look on the desk. Something familiar lies beneath the magnifying glass.

An old Mickey Mouse magazine is hidden among the maps and papers on the desk. Under the magnifying glass is Mickey!

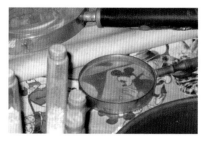

👉 **Indiana Jones Adventure:** When you come to the area with a rope that leads down a well, look at the design on the back of the raised well cover. Search the round border to find a Hidden Mickey.

A Hidden Mickey is . . . or was . . . in the lower right part of the well cover. As of this writing, the Hidden Mickey has been rubbed off as a result of so many people touching it, leaving only a smudge mark. But it could be back at anytime. Did you see it?

 Indiana Jones Adventure: As your ride vehicle speeds through a room lined with skeletons, look for a classic set of Mickey ears.

This one is really hard to find. You should be on the left side of the ride vehicle, ideally in the third row. Look back over your left shoulder for the best chance of spotting a skeleton wearing Mickey Mouse ears. Good luck!

 Tarzan's Treehouse: Work your way through the various rooms and watch for an old steamer trunk set in a corner. That's the key to finding this Mickey.

Metal rivets on either side of the keyhole form a Hidden Mickey.

 Walt Disney's Enchanted Tiki Room: The Hidden Mickey here moves around a lot and stays close to each Cast Member.

One of the shields on the shirts worn by Cast Members has a Hidden Mickey on it. The actual shield used to hang in the Enchanted Tiki Room. Politely ask a Cast Member to point it out.

NEW ORLEANS SQUARE

New Orleans Square was the first new land added to Disneyland after the original five. It is home to two of the most popular attractions: The Haunted Mansion and Pirates of the Caribbean. Walt Disney himself decided that Pirates should be a water ride. It was originally planned to be a wax museum!

👍 **The Haunted Mansion:** In the first room, just before the art gallery, take a look at those wall sconces holding the candles.

Stand at just the right angle and look up to see them form a perfect Hidden Mickey.

👍 **The Haunted Mansion:** As you walk through the dimly lit art gallery on the way to your Doom Buggy, take note of the elegant wallpaper.

Best seen near a light fixture, a classic Hidden Mickey is part of the wallpaper design.

👍 **The Haunted Mansion:** In the ballroom, scan the dinner table for a place setting in a recognizable shape.

A dinner plate and two side plates form a classic Hidden Mickey.

A REAL TUFFY **Pirates of the Caribbean:** After boarding a boat and entering the bayou, see if you can spot a Hidden Mickey floating on the water.

Look at the clusters of lily pads off the right side of the boat. They're hard to see, but three lily pads form the shape of Mickey's head.

 Pirates of the Caribbean: As your boat comes to the battle scene, look at the fort on the right, just under the cannons.

Again, this is dimly lit, but below the middle cannon you may be able to pick out a Mickey-shaped hole in the fortifications.

A REAL TUFFY **Pirates of the Caribbean:** In the last room before the exit, keep your eyes to the left. Check out the armor hanging on the wall.

Look left, at the pirate lying across a cannon. Now look to his far left at the pieces of armor hanging on the wall. One of them has a classic Hidden Mickey etched on the front. Good one!

Refreshment carts: These vending carts can be found throughout the park. It's fairly easy to get a handle on this classic Hidden Mickey.

Check the end of the metal bar used to pull the cart.

Walkway: On a wall near the shop called La Mascarade d'Orleans hangs a bronze plaque of a peacock. You'll have to look closely to find the Hidden Mickey.

A partial classic Hidden Mickey peeks out near the bottom of the peacock's tail.

CRITTER COUNTRY

The addition of Splash Mountain
in 1989 redefined this area of
the park, originally part of
Frontierland. Critter Country
encompasses Splash Mountain,
The Many Adventures of Winnie
the Pooh, Davy Crockett's
Explorer Canoes, and Hungry
Bear Restaurant, as well as some
critter-rific shops.

👍 **The Briar Patch gift shop:** Keep a sharp eye out for vegetables arranged in a certain order.

Three cabbages on a shelf behind the cash register form a Hidden Mickey.

 The Many Adventures of Winnie the Pooh: Upon first entering the attraction building, keep your eyes on the wood wall on the right.

A Hidden Mickey is etched in the grain of the wood.

👉 **The Many Adventures of Winnie the Pooh:** At the end of Pooh's dream, a classic Hidden Mickey is in the swirling painting of Heffalumps on the right.

Look below the Heffalump's trunk on the lower right. The Hidden Mickey is nearly upside down.

✋ **Splash Mountain:** There's no controversy about this Hidden Mickey. Examine the warning sign at the start of the standby line.

On the post below the sign, in the center, is a perfect Hidden Mickey stamped into a knothole.

👍 **Splash Mountain:** Where the queue enters the barn, look for a Hidden Mickey with small ears on an old machine.

Three gears comprise the shape of Mickey's head.

👉 **Splash Mountain:** On the ride, as you climb the last hill before the big drop, look at the roof of the tunnel above the highest point.

Rocks form a not-so-perfect shadowy profile of Mickey.

FRONTIERLAND

One of the most exciting areas of

the park, Frontierland celebrates

America's pioneering spirit. The

richly detailed *Mark Twain*, an

actual steam-powered paddleboat,

is a replica of the boats that plied

the Mississippi River in the 1800s.

Operating seasonally, the Sailing

Ship *Columbia* was first renovated

by Disney in the 1980s, having

been first constructed in 1787 in

Massachusetts.

Big Thunder Mountain Railroad: Along the fences outside the ride, and to the left of the exit, is a garden of cacti. There is one that really stands out.

Look for a cactus shaped like Mickey!

Big Thunder Mountain Railroad: As you ride the train, look to your left for a large Mickey formed by parts from a machine.

Three large gears are set together to make an upside-down Mickey.

Big Thunder Ranch: Find a big pile of horseshoes behind a fence. Could a Hidden Mickey be sitting there?

Three horseshoes form a creative Mickey. Giddyup!

 A REAL TUFFY **Big Thunder Ranch:** There are several hand-washing stations at the ranch. The one nearest the exit boasts a *very* Hidden Mickey.

Directly beneath the soap dispenser, three holes in the wooden tabletop make a Hidden Mickey. You might need to ask a Cast Member to help!

Frontierland Shootin' Exposition: A Frontierland favorite, this attraction features targets, including patches of prickly pear cacti.

Look near the tombstone marked NANCY'S DAN. There are several cacti that suggest the classic Hidden Mickey.

The Golden Horseshoe: Look over the posters that hang outside this frontier saloon.

To the left of the doors, a large poster contains vignettes of dancers. The border includes a flourish that reminds some people of Mickey's head—though the jury remains out on this one.

The Golden Horseshoe: A classic Hidden Mickey awaits you inside the restaurant. Search the front of the stage for this *grate* one!

Notice the ventilation grates on the front of the stage. Now look at the smaller one, in the middle. What you're looking for is in the lower right corner.

***Mark Twain* Riverboat:** As you leisurely ply the Rivers of America, take some time to stroll around the riverboat. From the bow on the upper deck, look up and wave to the captain in the wheelhouse. You'll be waving to something else, too.

Notice the ironwork between the two smokestacks, high above the deck. A sideways Mickey is part of the design. It's also visible from the stern.

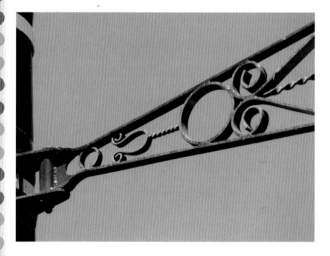

Rancho del Zocalo Restaurante: Once you've gotten your tray of food, you may want to stop at an island to pick up napkins, straws,

and other necessities. Before you leave, look around. A certain Mickey may make a real impression on you.

Look right at the wooden post near the wall. A classic Hidden Mickey is pressed into the wood. It's pretty subtle, but it's there. Keep looking!

River Belle Terrace: This elegantly themed restaurant features wall coverings decorated with birds, flowers, and berries.

Three berries create a classic Hidden Mickey that repeats as part of the pattern.

Tom Sawyer Island: Climb the tree house and look out toward the old mill. See if you can spot the Hidden Mickey looking back at you.

A Hidden Mickey is on the back of a chimney above the mill. Note: As of press time, Guests were no longer permitted to climb the tree house. Check if it is an option.

DISNEY CALIFORNIA ADVENTURE

BUENA VISTA STREET

The design of this welcoming avenue, named after the street on which Walt Disney Studios is located in Burbank, California, is inspired by the Los Angeles of 1923 (when Walt Disney stepped off the train from Kansas City, Missouri) through 1937 (with the premiere of *Snow White and the Seven Dwarfs*).

BEFORE YOU ENTER

If you're going to this park before you go to
Disneyland Park, check out the sections called Your
First Stop and Plaza in the Main Street, U.S.A. section,
under Disneyland Park. There are many Hidden
Mickeys outside the gates of Disney California
Adventure Park.

BUENA VISTA STREET

 Elias and Company advertisement: A
billboard-sized ad for Elias and Company,
painted on a brick wall near Oswald's,
contains a great Hidden Mickey.

> *Get close to the sign and look to the right
> of the N in OPEN. A perfect Mickey is
> part of the painted border. By the way,
> Elias is the name of Walt's father!*

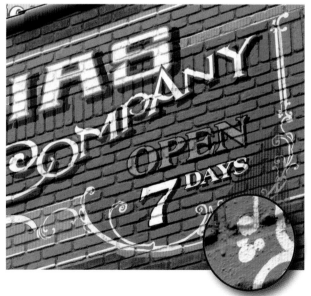

👍 **Clarabelle's Hand-Scooped Ice Cream:** Can you find a cow known as "Minnie Moo?"

Look for the milk jars on the shelves along the back wall behind the counter.

👆 **Julius Katz & Sons:** In a display window crowded with Mickey merchandise sits a clever Hidden Mickey. See if you can tune in to it.

A small TV has a Hidden Mickey shaped like a test pattern on its screen.

👆 **Julius Katz & Sons:** Walk around inside this interesting shop. Be sure to look up at the fans and other devices on the upper shelf.

The rollers of an old film splicer sitting near a fan form a Hidden Mickey.

👍 **Red Car Trolley:** A stone-faced Mickey waits at the first trolley stop.

The right side of the right pillar has a rock grouping familiar enough to ponder if it's an intentional Hidden Mickey.

 Trolley Treats: Inside the store, find the giant rock candy mountain that sits in a display window. Look inside the mountain through the opening behind a chocolate ladder. Good luck!

This is really tough to see, but inside the mountain is a snowman wearing Mickey ears. Talk about hidden!

HOLLYWOOD LAND

Ride the Red Car Trolley from

Buena Vista Street to old-time

Hollywood. Walt went from studio

to studio looking for a job as a film

director. But his first love was

animation, and when he got a

contract to produce a series of

cartoons ... well, the rest is history.

Disney's Aladdin—A Musical Spectacular: Take a careful look at the doorways within this theater.

On most of the exits, a painted frame outlines the door, featuring a gold Hidden Mickey in the top center.

Disney Animation: A Hidden Mickey sits somewhere on a flagpole in front of the animation building.

There is a classic Hidden Mickey at the top of the pole.

Disney Animation: If you go into the theater, look for a Hidden Mickey with a beat.

The drum set onstage is arranged to form a classic Hidden Mickey. Look around; the set includes other Mickeys, too.

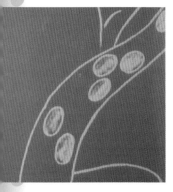

Disney Animation: In the exit hallway that leads from the theater, look for a line drawing of Ursula. See a Hidden Mickey anywhere?

Check out the tentacle on the right for an upside-down Mickey made of suction cups.

Disney Animation: In the Sorcerer's Workshop, there are several places you can find Hidden Mickeys. Begin by looking for two on the left wall. Then, move into The Beast's Library and find where he likes to get warm.

Mickey is in two wall medallions. One has a Sorcerer Mickey surrounded by a ring of large and small bubbles. They form several Hidden Mickeys.

Another medallion has a musical treble clef on it. Two circles to the left complete a Hidden Mickey turned counterclockwise.

The Beast warms himself in front of the fireplace. So does this Hidden Mickey!

☞ **Disney Animation:** Check out the **HAPPILY EVER AFTER** mural on your way out of the attraction.

Several Mickeys can be found in this wall mural. How many do you see?

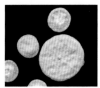

Mad T Party: You'll see many Mickeys at the House of Cards snack bar.

The backside of the card decorations house two Hidden Mickeys, and a nearby fence surrounding a smaller courtyard has a nice gold Mickey on the post. (You might get a better view of the fence from the outdoor queue of Monsters, Inc. Mike & Sulley to the Rescue!)

Monsters, Inc. Mike & Sulley to the Rescue!: As you go through the queue, there are several ads for the Monstropolis Cab Company with a graphic of a taxicab. There's something about those headlights.

A classic three-circle Hidden Mickey, rotated almost upside down, is on the front of the cab. You'll also see them as part of the video played on the monitors in the queue area.

A REAL TUFFY **Monsters, Inc. Mike & Sulley to the Rescue!:** During the ride, you'll come to a scene in which Boo is clobbering Randall. The lizardlike character changes color with each hit, but something else happens, too!

Every so often, a Hidden Mickey appears on Randall's belly, just above his lower leg.

A REAL TUFFY **Monsters, Inc. Mike & Sulley to the Rescue!:** Later on in the ride, on your left, you'll pass by Sulley holding a pink door. Take a look at the upper part of his left leg.

One of the dark blue spots in his fur is shaped liked Mickey's head.

Monsters, Inc. Mike & Sulley to the Rescue!: Just as the ride is ending, scan the control panel in the back of the news van.

Dials and gauges form a recognizable three-circle Mickey.

Muppet★Vision 3D: In the preshow space, go all the way to the front to find this brassy Hidden Mickey.

Toward the bottom right side, a pink suitcase features a metallic lock that resembles those classic three circles.

Muppet★Vision 3D: After the cannon blasts a hole through the theater's wall, search the crowd of people for a Hidden Mickey.

Several park Guests are holding Mickey Mouse balloons, and at least one is wearing mouse ears.

Off the Page store: Outside, find the Dalmatians in a display window. They have spots, you know.

One adorable pup has an upside-down Mickey on his knee.

Off the Page store: Inside, animation drawings hang from the ceiling. Look for the crocodile. A Hidden Mickey is bubbling up.

Three bubbles next to the shadow of the croc's claw form a slightly distorted, sideways Mickey.

Red Car Trolley: At the trolley's last stop, by The Twilight Zone Tower of Terror, there's a large gate with a billboard advertising the Red Car Trolley. Two Mickeys are hidden there.

On the lower right, there's a postcard illustration of Paradise Pier. One Mickey is on the hub of the Ferris wheel. The other is his upside-down reflection on the water!

Schmoozies: If you stop for a fruit smoothie, or even if you don't, be sure to check out the fabulous wall mosaics. There are plenty of possible Mickeys here. One is near a word that describes what you do when you're hungry.

To the right of three tiles with the letters E, A, and T is a classic Hidden Mickey with buttons for ears. See if you can find other ones, too!

The Twilight Zone Tower of Terror: Once inside the building, a video plays as an introduction to the ride. Mickey makes an unexpected appearance!

The little girl is holding a Mickey Mouse doll. You'll see her and the doll when you're on the ride, too.

The Twilight Zone Tower of Terror: After the video, walk up the stairs to examine the cage before continuing onto to your elevator bay.

A Hidden Mickey made of a warming cover and two serving trays sits on the cage floor, directly facing the staircase.

 The Twilight Zone Tower of Terror: Position yourself so you can board the elevators upstairs and on the left. If you do, you may find an illuminated Hidden Mickey there.

As you wait for the elevators on the left, look up at the grate above you. Spotlights shining down on the grate make a Hidden Mickey.

The Twilight Zone Tower of Terror: Search the gift shop for a framed photo of the family featured in the ride. What's that in the little girl's hands?

She's holding a Mickey Mouse plush doll.

The Twilight Zone Tower of Terror: Also in the gift shop, there are a number of old cameras on display. Several have lenses and viewfinder windows arranged in a fashion that kind of resembles Mickey. But one particular box camera stands out.

A camera in the middle of a corner shelf has a lens in the center that could be Mickey's head, although the "ears" are not in the right proportion.

"A BUG'S LAND"

This land, which opened in 2002, was the first expansion of Disney California Adventure Park. Based on the movie *"a bug's life,"* it gives Guests a unique bug's-eye view of the world. In fact, amid the towering clover and telephone pole-sized pencils, you'll feel as though you've been shrunk to the size of a bug!

Fun & Fruity Drink stand: An easy-to-find Hidden Mickey graces this food cart.

Three cherries on the menu form a Hidden Mickey that children of all ages will be able to spot, while a different cherry cluster on the stand's outer left wall also resembles our intrepid mouse.

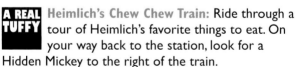

A REAL TUFFY **Heimlich's Chew Chew Train:** Ride through a tour of Heimlich's favorite things to eat. On your way back to the station, look for a Hidden Mickey to the right of the train.

In a bank of dirt, three rocks form a Hidden Mickey. They are just to the right of a large root.

It's Tough to be a Bug!: Find two Hidden Mickeys made of hollow stalks high up in this theater.

Look on the walls near the second set of exit doors from the stage. Among moss, they roost in the upper rock formations on both sides of the theater.

CARS LAND

Home to Lightning McQueen, Mater, and all of their pals, Cars Land was built as part of the massive reimagining of Disney California Adventure Park, and opened in June 2012. The multi-hued hills of Ornament Valley not only serve as the picturesque setting for Radiator Springs Racers, but they also screen out structures outside of the park.

👍 **Fire Department:** Stand facing the front of the Fire Department. There is a Hidden Mickey made from wire loops nearby!

Up on the power line to your left is a great classic Hidden Mickey.

🚗 **Luigi's Flying Tires:** In the queue for this fun ride, there are collections of racing memorabilia on the wall behind glass. Check the third collage from the right for a special antenna topper.

A Lightning McQueen antenna topper is wearing Mickey ears.

👉 **Luigi's Flying Tires:** In the fourth collage of memorabilia from the right, look for Mickey hidden on the front of a vehicle.

A three-circle Mickey, rotated a quarter turn clockwise, forms the headlights of a car.

A REAL TUFFY **Radiator Springs Curios shop:** A wonderful Hidden Mickey is located on the porch of this shop.

On the far left wall, under the window, is a yellow sign that reads PUMP. Look straight down on it from above to see Mickey on the top right edge.

👍 **Radiator Springs Curios shop:** Walk into the store and examine the pattern on the ceiling.

In the center is a round medallion with smaller circles that appear to be ears.

Radiator Springs Curios shop: Somewhere inside the shop is a yellow sign with two red ears!

Look to the right of the cashier. The sign says SERVICE.

Radiator Springs Racers: In the standby queue area, look to your right for a Hidden Mickey composed of three plants.

Three cacti are arranged in the familiar classic Hidden Mickey.

Radiator Springs Racers: Later in the queue, inside Stanley's Cap 'n Tap, is a picture of a bride and groom. The bride's veil is especially lovely!

Three gears in the center of the veil make a Hidden Mickey, though the "ear" gears are a bit small.

Radiator Springs Racers: As you pass through The Amazing Oil Bottle House, you may be able to pick out several Hidden Mickeys. Outside, along the back wall, is a good place to look.

Most of the bottles are spaced too far apart, but there are a few exceptions!

Radiator Springs Racers: If your race car goes through Ramone's House of Body Art, turn to look at the right rear wall.

Look for an electrical box with a three-circle Mickey on it.

 Ramone's House of Body Art: You'll want to spend time at this location in Radiator Springs. There are wonderful Hidden Mickeys here! To get started, look at the six beautifully painted car hoods in the display windows. Each one has a Hidden Mickey on it! Some are easy to spot; others are really tough. Good luck!

Starting on the right, check out the hood with a geometric design. Mickey is in a yellow section.

The hood with yellow and orange flames has a Hidden Mickey in the orange section on the upper right side.

On the brown hood with pinstriping, Mickey is near the bottom center, where two curved pinstripes meet.

A white-and-blue hood with orange edging has a Hidden Mickey on the right side, in the orange stripe.

The hood with wings and fire in the center has a Hidden Mickey in the flames. It's very hard to pick out!

*On the car hood with lace work, look
in the lower center section of lace.*

Ramone's House of Body Art: Inside, behind the
cash register, is one more car hood. This one has a
Hidden Mickey that is a bit easier to spot.

*Look on the right side of the hood,
in the darker purple color.*

**Ramone's House of Body
Art:** The merchandise area has a
very cool logo painted on
wooden posts.

*The logo contains a
perfect classic Hidden
Mickey, somewhat
hidden in the design.*

**Ramone's House of
Body Art:** Some merchandise
is displayed on purple boxes.

*Move around until you can
see the side of the box. A
classic Hidden Mickey
design is hiding there.*

Welcome to Cars Land sign: At the foot of the
sign is a cactus garden. See if you can pick out a
Hidden Mickey there.

*Three cacti form an upside-down Mickey. The cactus
representing Mickey's head is taller than his ears.*

PACIFIC WHARF

Reminiscent of Cannery Row in
Monterey, the Pacific Wharf is
packed with restaurants. It's a
great place to get a taste of
California. You can sample a
freshly baked piece of sourdough
bread, indulge in a square of
Ghirardelli chocolate, sip a
margarita, or snack on a taco.

👍 **The Bakery Tour:** As you walk through this working bakery, keep an eye out for a raised Hidden Mickey or two.

Bread loaves in the shape of Mickey's head are often seen on the tour and within the Pacific Wharf Cafe. They are sometimes also sold at a nearby cart.

👎 **Golden Vine Winery:** Walking from the park's main entrance, turn right onto a pathway along a small vineyard to unearth this small Hidden Mickey.

Within an informational plaque on white wines, find a perfectly proportioned three-circle cluster of purple grapes by PINOT GRIGIO.

A REAL TUFFY **Walt Disney Imagineering Blue Sky Cellar Preview Center:** There's something quite magical, and mousy, about the pixie dust on this main outdoor sign.

Find a Hidden Mickey near a bigger star on the lower left-hand side.

👍 **World of Color nighttime spectacular:** At the end of a scene with the characters from *Up*, watch as the balloons float upward. Anything familiar?

After the house passes by, a singular Mickey-shaped balloon takes center screen.

PARADISE PIER

California's coastline was dotted with small amusement parks and piers in the late 1920s. Paradise Pier pays tribute to that heritage. The roller coaster, California Screamin', is built in the style of the old wooden coasters, but this one launches riders up the first hill at nearly sixty miles per hour!

Ariel's Grotto restaurant: Go downstairs, and see if Mickey bubbles up.

On the wall almost directly facing the stairs, look to a lower left-hand corner to spy a Hidden Mickey made of three bubbles.

Bathroom and telephone outdoor hallway: Look up to see Mickey eavesdropping.

Find a Hidden Mickey in the corners of the white metalwork holding the signs.

Billboard: On the walkway that leads to California Screamin' is a large billboard for Paradise Pier. Check out the beach umbrellas.

Three umbrellas on the lower right make a pretty good classic Hidden Mickey.

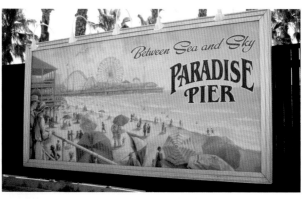

 California Screamin': This high-speed coaster takes you upside down through a loop. Keep your eyes open and you may be rewarded!

Look straight down from the top of the loop. One of the concrete footings below is shaped like Mickey's head. Talk about hidden!

Cover Bar: Take a seat, and look for Mickey.

*Most of the white metal chair backs
feature a classic Hidden Mickey.*

Gazebo: As you walk toward the boardwalk, take a look at the gazebo near the Cove Bar. Its lifesaving equipment is in fine shape!

*Three life preservers form
a perfect three-circle Mickey.
Flags, curtains, and a lightning
rod on top all feature an
anchor with Mickey ears.*

Goofy's Sky School: The sign for Goofy's school is up on the roof, but parts of it seem to be missing.

*Three holes in the billboard roughly
form a sideways Mickey.*

Goofy's Sky School: As you work your way through the queue, look for bulletin boards. Mickey has made a good impression on them!

*A small, classic Hidden Mickey is
indented on each bulletin board.*

The Little Mermaid——Ariel's Undersea Adventure: Graceful iron scrollwork of waves and bubbles adorns the building.

*A pattern of three
adjacent bubbles makes
a great Mickey. The
pattern repeats above
the arches.*

The Little Mermaid—Ariel's Undersea Adventure: Once in your "clam-mobile," look at the mural that runs the length of the wall. A rockin' Mickey can be found there.

On the far left, a few inches above the wall tiles, the rock features a three-circle Mickey.

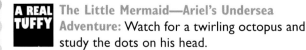

A REAL TUFFY **The Little Mermaid—Ariel's Undersea Adventure:** Watch for a twirling octopus and study the dots on his head.

In the "Under the Sea" scene, three pink spots on the octopus's head form a sideways three-circle Mickey.

The Little Mermaid—Ariel's Undersea Adventure: Ariel needs a kiss to remain human, but it has to be the kiss of true love from Eric—no frogs!

The frogs in the "Kiss the Girl" scene have spots that resemble Mickey's head on their backs.

Man Hat N' Beach: Find the eight-legged critter wearing a sailor hat and see if you can spot something special.

Three orange spots on the back of the octopus's head converge in the shape of Mickey's head.

Meet Duffy the Disney Bear pavilion: This photo location sports several Hidden Mickeys. Can you spot all three?

Banners on the support posts are emblazoned with Duffy's paw print. A classic Hidden Mickey is part of the design.

Other banners have an anchor pictured. See Mickey?

Inside the pavilion, two portholes and a ship's wheel make one more Hidden Mickey.

Point Mugu Tattoo: Search the four walls for your favorite hidden mouse.

Look up on the back wall, between the words "Paradise" and "Pier."

Point Mugu Tattoo: You're not done yet! One more Hidden Mickey is waiting to be found. Surf's up!

Mickey is hidden in the DCA flaming surfboard art.

Paradise Pier Amusement Co. game stand: Scan the outside of this building for two Hidden Mickeys hiding in plain sight.

Look up at the scrollwork beneath the roof peak. Two tilted Hidden Mickeys decorate the eaves.

Seaside Souvenirs: This open-air shop has a lovely mural behind the cash register.

A Mickey Mouse balloon appears in each of the far corners of the painting.

Sideshow Shirts store: Find the painting of pistol-totin' Betty Ducks. Legend has it she was framed!

There's a Hidden Mickey on the right side of the picture frame.

Sideshow Shirts store: In the front of the store is a man lying on a bed of nails. A great Hidden Mickey is there, too.

Mickey is just about in the middle of the wooden bed frame.

Toy Story Midway Mania!: While waiting in line, set your sights for the Dino Darts poster. See if you can find a Hidden Mickey there. *Bullseye!*

Three spots on Trixie the triceratops form a slightly distorted Mickey.

Toy Story Midway Mania!: Check out the art in the loading area. Look for three picture frames that make a Hidden Mickey.

Three oval vignettes on the right form a really big Hidden Mickey.

Toy Story Midway Mania!: As you exit the ride, you'll go through Andy's room. Look at the game box on the rug.

It features the same art as the loading area. Three oval frames make the Hidden Mickey.

Toy Story Midway Mania!: Find a beverage stand just across from this attraction, and try to find some news on Mickey.

From a tall height, look down at the front pages of fake newspaper stacks to see Steamboat Willie.

👉 **Treasures in Paradise shop:** You'll find at least four Hidden Mickeys in this shop. For starters, find the lion.

Mickey's head bedecks the lion's saddle.

👉 **Treasures in Paradise shop:** Search the store for a painting of a female illusionist. A Hidden Mickey is part of her costume.

Her round belt buckle forms the head, with the ears on the belt above. Not a perfect Mickey, but pretty good. What do you think?

👉 **Treasures in Paradise shop:** Duffy the Disney Bear is everywhere! See if you can find something special about his face.

The outline of his face forms a Hidden Mickey!

👉 **Treasures in Paradise shop:** Plush Duffy Bears line the shelves. What else do you notice about Duffy?

The bottoms of Duffy's feet have Mickey-shaped pads on them.

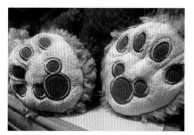

GRIZZLY PEAK

California's natural beauty and recreational opportunities are celebrated here. The centerpiece, Grizzly Peak, takes the form of California's state animal: the grizzly bear. Grizzly Peak is home to Grizzly River Run, the world's tallest, longest, and fastest rapids ride!

Grizzly River Run: From Paradise Pier, walk to the attraction entrance via the far right path. Once you pass a right-hand sign for the **EUREKA MINE SHAFT NO. 2**, stop and look across to the left. Can you find the perfect spot to spy Mickey?

The view of this Hidden Mickey gear crank goes from good to better to best, depending on exactly where you stand.

A REAL TUFFY **Redwood Creek Challenge Trail:** Take a look at the colorful trail map and the entrance of this attraction. Find three Hidden Mickeys on the left side. Can you find them all?

Starting in the top left corner of the map, three rocks in the river suggest the shape of Mickey's head.

Moving down to the middle left, check out the foaming water at the base of a hollow log.

Below that, in the camp circle, look for three log stools arranged just so.

Redwood Creek Challenge Trail: Enjoy the challenge trail and take note of any Hidden Mickeys you find. A good one lies at the entrance to a cave.

Find Kenai's Spirit Cave and look in the shallow creek at the entrance. Faux stepping-stones are arranged in the shape of Mickey's head.

Rushin' River Outfitters: This camp store has everything a gold prospector needs to strike it rich. On the shelves are critters that leave a distinctive paw print.

The plush grizzly bear cubs have Mickey-shaped pads on their paws.

CONDOR FLATS

California's aviation industry played an important role in the state's economic development. Condor Flats salutes the pioneering aviators that led the way. To get a bird's-eye view of all the state has to offer, take a ride on Soarin' Over California.

Refreshment carts: As in Disneyland Park, carts selling ice cream, drinks, and snacks can be found throughout the park. Look for a classic Hidden Mickey made of metal.

Mickey can be found at the end of the metal bar used to pull the cart.

A REAL TUFFY **Soarin' Over California:** As you fly over a golf course, a ball is hit right toward you. Keep your eyes on it!

The ball rotates to reveal a Hidden Mickey.

 **Soarin' Over California:** Immediately after the ball flies by, look for a Hidden Mickey among the people on the golf course.

One of them is holding a Mickey Mouse balloon.

Soarin' Over California: Enjoy the fireworks in the final scene and see if you can pick out one more Hidden Mickey.

Watch for the second burst of fireworks. The one in the middle of the screen forms the head, and two smaller bursts make the ears.

Taste Pilots' Grill: The dining area has a number of interesting framed photos of historic aircraft and engines. One looks a bit mousy.

In one photo, an early jet engine seems to be wearing Mickey ears! There are two identical pictures in the dining area. One is to the left of the food pickup area and the other is on the right, rear wall.

REST OF
THE RESORT

DOWNTOWN DISNEY DISTRICT

Forty-five years after the
dedication of Disneyland, the
opening of Disney California
Adventure in 2001 marked a new
era for the Disneyland Resort—a
complex of two parks, three
hotels, and the Downtown Disney
entertainment district. Today,
Downtown Disney, with its lively
mix of restaurants, shops, and
entertainment venues, is a
destination of its own.

A REAL TUFFY **Disney Vault 28:** This hip store has great Hidden Mickeys inside, but there's an even better one right before you go in. Start by examining the bricks to the right of the right display window.

A terrific Hidden Mickey is part of the brickwork. Did you spot it?

👍 **Disney Vault 28:** Now, stand at the entrance and take a look at the large metal vault door. Hidden Mickeys are high and low.

Two Hidden Mickeys, one at the top right and the other on the bottom right (upside down) are riveted to the door.

👣 **Disney Vault 28:** Inside there are a number of Hidden Mickeys done in a graffiti art style. Some are obvious, but others are hidden by merchandise or art.

Look for a mouse-ified skull-and-crossbones design. Search around the store to see how many more Hidden Mickeys you can find. The best-kept secret is the one on a street-facing air duct up high, between the two doorways.

👉 **D Street:** Look for graffiti-style Mickey Mouse images painted on the walls in each of rooms. Can you find the Hidden Mickey within one of them?

In the second room, look for Mickey wearing a belt. The belt buckle has a Hidden Mickey.

👉 **D Street:** Take a look behind the cash register for a Hidden Mickey among the artwork.

The section of exposed brick behind the artwork is shaped like Mickey's head.

👉 **Kiosks:** Retail kiosks line the Downtown Disney District. Take note of their decorative ironwork.

Hidden Mickeys appear in the eaves and on top of the kiosks.

👉 **Marceline's Confectionery:** There's a sweet Hidden Mickey in this sign.

Look at the curl of the font between the M and C. It's a perfect Hidden Mickey.

👉 **Studio Disney 365:** A child's changing room mirror might offer some Mickey magic.

There are at least four Hidden Mickeys formed from jewels on the mirror's frame. Note: As of press time, construction on Anna & Elsa's Boutique began in this space. Check if the Hidden Mickeys remained!

 World of Disney: Check out the sign above this busy store. Two Hidden Mickeys reside there.

Blue Mickey heads sit on top of the scrolls that hold the sign.

On the sign nearest to Starbucks, look at the gold metal knob in the center for an extra-discreet Hidden Mickey.

A REAL TUFFY **World of Disney:** Artwork of characters and scenery run along the top of the walls. Look for the picture of Goofy steering a gondola with Mickey and Minnie aboard.

To the left of Goofy, a Hidden Mickey decorates the arch above the middle of the bridge.

World of Disney: Now find the picture of Mickey, Minnie, Goofy, and the Dalmatians outside of Hollywood's famed Chinese theater.

> *A classic Hidden Mickey is in a medallion at the top of the theater's entrance.*

👆 **World of Disney:** In the same room, look at the blown map behind the cash register.

> *There are two more Hidden Mickeys on the ends of the scroll.*

👍 **World of Disney:** Outside, the awnings above most windows are noteworthy.

> *While fairly large and obvious, these Hidden Mickeys present a challenge in that you have to look up high to spot them.*

THE RESORTS

In recent years, the plans for developing the Disneyland Resort included renovating two hotels—Disney's Paradise Pier Hotel and the Disneyland Hotel. A new hotel, Disney's Grand Californian Hotel & Spa, was also built in the style of the Arts & Crafts movement of the early twentieth century. It's the first Disney hotel to be located inside a park. Guests have a private entrance into Disney California Adventure.

DISNEY'S GRAND CALIFORNIAN HOTEL & SPA

👆 **Entrance:** The hotel logo incorporates a classic Hidden Mickey, and it is used in many creative ways throughout the hotel. Look for the colorful tile panels by the main entrance and see if you can find Mickey.

Mickey is in the tree, just above the tree's trunk.

 Entrance: Near the valet window, find the tiles that portray a big tree with smaller trees behind it. You shouldn't have any trouble spotting Hidden Mickeys here!

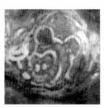

The tiles have as many as nine Hidden Mickeys. An etching of Mickey's three-quarter profile is the toughest to spot.

👆 **Front desk:** Many Hidden Mickeys await you here. Some are in the fabric wall hangings behind the front desk. Check out the one on the far left!

The Hidden Mickey sits just above the trunk of the first tree on the left.

 Front desk: In the center of the main registration desk, look for a tiled picture of three dancing bears. And a few Hidden Mickeys, too!

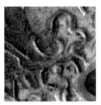

There's a Hidden Mickey in a tree to the left of the bears, but the best is near the foot of a brown bear: it's an etching of Mickey holding a conductor's baton.

👉 **Front desk:** You'll see more artistic tiles placed all along the registration desk off to the far left. Look for one in a tree to the right of three dancing bears.

A brown classic Hidden Mickey is on the lower part of the tree.

👉 **Guest rooms:** If you're staying in a Guest room, look down!

The pattern of the carpeting in the Guest rooms includes Mickey.

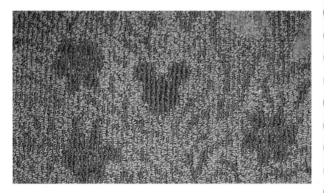

👉 **Hallway to conference center:** As you enter this corridor, pay attention to the framed art on the walls.

Actually, pay more attention to the frames than the art!

Classic Hidden Mickeys anchor the corners of several frames.

👉 **Hearthstone Lounge:** Soft lighting makes the lounge an inviting place to relax.

The light fixtures have holes shaped like Mickey's head.

👍 **Lamps:** Along walkways, such as the one that leads to Disney California Adventure Park, large lamps sit on brick posts. Look for Mickey in the metalwork.

There is a Mickey-shaped opening in the tree on the right, just above the trunk.

✌ **Lobby:** Find the grandfather clock and stand facing it. See anything?

A classic Mickey shape is hammered into the clockface.

A REAL TUFFY

Lobby: A big wooden desk is decorated with a Hidden Mickey. You're more likely to find it if you're not too tall!

Look under the front edge of the desk.

Lobby: Just off the lobby, a map of the hotel grounds depicts a very interesting structure.

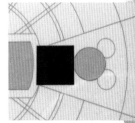

Look for the children's swimming pool. It has ears!

Lobby fireplace: Inside and outside mantels made of rocks offer fairly good Hidden Mickeys. Inside, look for a large formation on the left side of the main fireplace. Then exit the lobby through the left-side doors nearest to you. Take a look at the rock wall on your right.

Inside, one of the larger boulders on the floor has what looks like perfectly placed mouse ears.

Outside, a smaller, higher-up Hidden Mickey features the ears a bit closer together.

DISNEY'S PARADISE PIER HOTEL

👈 **Disney's PCH Grill:** Check out the panels in the doors to the restaurant.

The bottom left panel of the door on the right side features a partial Mickey. Keep your eyes open inside the restaurant for other Hidden Mickeys!

👉 **Game room:** Video games positioned along the walls are separated by tall partitions with decorative tops.

The tops of the partitions are carved in the shape of a half-Mickey.

👆 **Guest rooms:** Find at least four styles of Hidden Mickeys in most rooms.

A Hidden Mickey is stained into a wooden panel by the closet.

The outline of Mickey is stained into the wooden desktop.

Lighthouse lamps on the desk feature lampshades with a row of Hidden Mickeys.

Most standard rooms will have a green bed runner with white circles; look closer at the repeating pattern to see Mickey's head.

👈 **Guest room hallways:** The carpet pattern should be quite familiar.

A small, white Hidden Mickey is worked into the design of the hallway carpets.

👉 **Hotel, front entrance:** Find a marble wall off to the left of the entrance for several Hidden Mickeys.

Gloss paint designs form the outlines, not full circles, of classic Hidden Mickeys on various rectangle titles.

👉 **Hotel, rear entrance:** The Hidden Mickeys here are lined up and hard to miss. Can you spot them?

Posts along the driveway are topped with classic Hidden Mickeys.

👉 **Lobby, elevators:** Keep an eye out for Mickey when you ride the elevator.

Inside the elevator cars, there are surfboards painted on the walls. Some include Hidden Mickeys in their patterns.

Lobby, hallway: Halfway down the hall that goes from front to back hangs a painting with the words HOT DOG on it. Take a look!

On both sides of the words are classic Hidden Mickey designs that can be viewed both right side up and upside down. See them?

Lobby, map: Find the wall map of the property and look for the **YOU ARE HERE** symbol. Who else is there?

A classic Hidden Mickey, of course!

Mickey's Beach Fitness Center: Study this entranceway for at least three different types of Hidden Mickeys

The top corners of the wooden doorframe each have a die-cut design.

The windows on each door are shaped like Mickey.

Through the windows, you can see to the far wall, which also features die-cut wood reminiscent of the mouse.

👆 **Pacific Ballroom, hallway:** Across from the ballroom doors, find the picture of an ocean sunset.

A classic Hidden Mickey appears as a reflection of light off of the water.

👆 **Paradise Pool:** See any Hidden Mickeys swimming up here?

A row of metallic Hidden Mickeys is part of the design in the fence around the pool area.

DISNEYLAND HOTEL

👍 **Carpets:** Notice the details down low to find Hidden Mickeys throughout the hotel.

In Disney's Fantasia Shop near the main lobby, look for a nice profile of Mickey in blue.

At the Convention Center entrance nearest to the lobby, see a large gold Hidden Mickey.

Look closer at that carpet's edging throughout the hall to find smaller gold Hidden Mickeys on blue.

In the Convention Center's second-floor hallways, look for gold Hidden Mickeys on red.

Within the ballrooms, including the elegant Sleeping Beauty Pavilion, look for a swirly classic Hidden Mickey.

In all guest rooms, notice similar elegant, and mousy, designs.

👎 **Convention center, ballroom walls:** Find Mickey all in gold.

The divider walls of each ballroom feature a pattern similar to the hallway carpets.

☞ **Convention center, ceiling:** To find these Hidden Mickeys, you'll need to shed some light on the subject.

Look up at the parasol-shaped light fixtures. Hidden Mickeys are included in several of the designs.

☞ **Convention center, stairs:** Just to be safe, hold on to the handrails while going up and down the stairs.

At the tops and bases of the stairs, the handrail swirls around a finial shaped like Mickey's head.

☞ **Convention center, second-floor hallway:** Find the public telephones across from the ballrooms. Mickey lights the way!

Mickey's profile is painted on the glass panels that separate the phones.

The shade on the lamp above the phone emits light through holes shaped like the outline of Mickey's head.

👉 **Convention center, second-floor hallway:** Find the hotel house phone, and you'll find another Hidden Mickey.

> *Look for a classic Hidden Mickey with a question mark on it, just above the bottom row of buttons.*

👆 **Convention center, second-floor hallway:** A Mickey's Toontown-concept painting hangs near the ballrooms. Can you find two Hidden Mickeys in it?

> *In the lower right corner, two children are wearing Mickey Mouse ears.*

 Convention center, second-floor hallway: Another painting shows adventurers at a jungle temple. Take a look at their vehicle.

> *A Hidden Mickey is part of the vehicle's hood ornament.*

👏 **Convention center, second-floor hallway:** Next, look for a concept painting of Splash Mountain. Three different Hidden Mickeys have found their "laughing place" here.

> *Notice the family in the shade facing the attraction to find a red Mickey-shaped balloon.*

> *Find the family of three; the little boy is holding another Mickey Mouse balloon.*

> *Look to the far right to see the child wearing mouse ears.*

Convention center, Sleeping Beauty Pavilion: Ready to relax after walking around the parks? Take a load off—and look for Mickey if you're so inclined.

Perfect, classic Hidden Mickeys are part of the chair's fabric design.

 Disney Cruise Line model: In all three of the hotel's main lobbies, find a model of the *Fantasy*. Can you find any Hidden Mickeys there?

Check the stacks, the bow, and the bottom of the pool!

A REAL TUFFY **Fantasy Tower, elevators:** Stand inside facing the doors, look to the left, and see if Mickey is reflected.

A Hidden Mickey hides in plain sight among the stars and other etchings.

 Frontier Tower, driveway gate: Upon entering the tower from the Downtown Disney parking lot, notice a driveway gate off to the right.

A large Hidden Mickey rests in the center of the gate.

Frontier Tower, lobby: There are many nice round places to sit, arranged in groups of three.

Round, padded stools are grouped together to make perfect Hidden Mickeys.

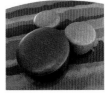

A REAL TUFFY **Frontier Tower, lobby:** Down a hallway that leads from the lobby is a painting of an old western street scene. Look for a familiar pattern.

The woman's skirt is dotted with what hint towards classic Hidden Mickeys.

 **Frontier Tower, lobby:** On a door marked for Cast Members, near the old western scene, some of a Hidden Mickey peeks out from above the door handle.

Made from a mirrored plate, a small circle and quarter circle form a clearly intentional, but partially Hidden Mickey.

👆 **Frontier Tower, lobby:** Halfway down the hallway from the lobby, see a staircase off to the left. On the middle landing, take a second look at the wall's

artwork.

Look just above the words MULE PACK RIDE to see a child wearing mouse ears.

👆 **Goofy's Kitchen:** Go up the stairs to the left of the restaurant's entrance. A huge and obvious Mickey hangs from the ceiling. But several not-so-obvious Hidden Mickeys surround it.

Small Hidden Mickeys anchor the light fixture's wires to the ceiling.

👆 **Guest room bathrooms:** You'll see plenty of subtle, and obvious, touches from the mouse.

The lights around the main mirror are "held" by Mickey's hands; the lampshades also have an understated classic Hidden Mickey pattern.

A separate light fixture features Mickey in the metal design.

The shower and sink faucet handles have mouse ears on the edges.

Guest room desk lamps: There's something familiar about the base.

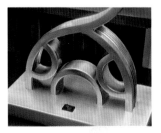

A Hidden Mickey, formed by two smaller circles and a bigger half circle, is part of the metal design.

Guest room headboards: In most rooms, look closer at the wooden-etched design of Sleeping Beauty Castle and fireworks.

Off to the left, notice that three fireworks form a Hidden Mickey.

Hotel maps: Forgot to pick up a map at the front desk? Never fear. Throughout the towers, there are ones with a distinct mouselike quality.

On the map of the hotel grounds, the hot tub near the main pool has "ears."

👆 **Mickey Mouse Penthouse:** As the name of this glamorous signature suite would imply, Mickey is everywhere. One of the largest, most-innovative elements is in the ceiling.

A (sort of) Hidden Mickey is formed within the color changing mood-lighting fixture in the living room.

👆 **Poolside hot tub:** This is technically a Hidden Minnie, but it's too good not to mention.

Mouse ears and the signature polka dot bow have been painted on the grounds surrounding this circular tub.

INDEX

Editorial Director: Wendy Lefkon
Editor: Jennifer Eastwood

Designer: H. Clark Wakabayashi

This book's producers would like to thank Jennifer Black, Monique Diman, Dennis Ely, Winnie Ho, Alan Kaplan, Warren Meislin, Betsy Mercer, Scott Piehl, Steve Plotkin, Chip Poakeart, Michael Serrian, Betsy Singer, Muriel Tebid, Marybeth Tregarthen, Dushawn Ward, and Jessie Ward.

ISBN 978-1-4847-1276-4
FAC-029191-16152
Printed in Malaysia
First Paperback Edition, April 2015
10 9 8 7 6 5 4 3

Visit www.disneybooks.com

The Official Disney Fan Club

D23.com

PHOTO CREDITS: Photography by JENNIFER EASTWOOD on front cover (top: bark notch, full-body sign, white sign, balloon, turnstile, streetlamp, bell; bottom: profile-shaped continent, mailbox), back cover (left: rivet, horseshoes; right: grapes, cactus), and pages 5, 10, 12, 13 (except signpost), 14, 15, 17 (except Plaza Inn), 20 (except vase), 21 (Mad Hatter Shop), 22, 23, 24 (close-up), 25 (except ship), 28 (Entrance Gate), 29 (*My Life with Walt*), 31 (drum), 32 (picture frame), 33 (except signpost), 34, 36 (except Autopia car), 37, 38 (rug), 39, 40, 41, 45 (lock), 48 (sconce), 51, 52, 54, 56 (ironwork), 57 (close-up), 62, 63 (except film splicer), 66 (pole), 67 (Sorcerer Mickey, mural), 68 (Mad T Party), 69 (except Dalmatian), 73 (top), 76 (PUMP sign), 77 (ceiling, cactus), 78, 81, 84 (Ariel's Grotto), 86 (banner), 87 (balloons), 88 (Sideshow Shirts), 89 (Duffy sign), 92 (gear crank, rocks), 93 (bear), 95 (except Taste Pilots' Grill), 96–97, 98, 100, 101 (except kiosks), 102, 103, 106 (except hotel logo), 108 (clock), 109, 110 (game room), 111 (carpet, surfboard), 112 (except map), 113 (door, pool), 114, 115 (except parasols), 116, 117, 118, 119 (except bathroom), and 120 (map); BILL SCOLLON front cover (top: carpet, gem with buttons; bottom: stones, gold frame, life preservers), back cover (left: ironwork; right: signpost design), and on pages 13 (signpost), 16, 17 (except Plaza Inn), 20 (vase), 21 (King Arthur Carrousel), 24 (except close-up), 25, (ship), 28 (Clarabelle's Frozen Yogurt), 29 (except *My Life with Walt*), 30, 31 (except drum), 32 (car), 33 (signpost), 36 (Autopia car), 38 (except rug), 44, 45 (shirt), 49. 55, 56 (grate), 57 (except close-up), 63 (film splicer), 66 (Ursula), 67 (treble clef and fireplace), 68 (cab), 69 (Dalmatian), 70, 71, 73 (except top), 76 (except PUMP sign), 77 (wall, bottles), 79, 84 (billboard), 85, 86 (mural), 87 (except balloons), 88 (except Sideshow Shirts), 89 (except Duffy sign), 92 (foaming water, camp circle), 93 (cave), 95 (Taste Pilots' Grill), 101 (kiosks), 106 (hotel logo), 107, 111 (posts), 112 (map), 113 (sunset), and 115 (parasols).

The Haunted Mansion wallpaper (page 48) courtesy of the Walt Disney Imagineering Art Collection.

A NOTE FROM THE BOOK'S PRODUCERS: Do you see an entry in this book that you don't think should count as a true Hidden Mickey? That's fair! Identifying Hidden Mickeys is a subjective pastime. To date, no official list exists on what truly counts as a Hidden Mickey, so don't use this book as the official guide. It's one interpretative version of this fun hobby, and we hope you enjoy it!

READER'S FINDS

In your travels through the Disneyland Resort, you might come across a Hidden Mickey or two not listed in this book. After all, the parks and resorts are always changing! Describe them here. Happy hunting!

_____

_____

_____

_____

_____

_____

_____

_____

_____

_____

_____

_____

_____

_____

_____

_____

_____

_____

_____

_____

_____

_____

_____